ENDANGERED AND THREATENED ANIMALS

THE RHINO

A MyReportLinks.com Book

Jan M. Czech

MyReportLinks.com Books

an imprint of

 Enslow Publishers, Inc.

Box 398, 40 Industrial Road
Berkeley Heights, NJ 07922
USA

MyReportLinks.com Books, an imprint of Enslow Publishers, Inc. MyReportLinks®
is a registered trademark of Enslow Publishers, Inc.

Library of Congress Cataloging-in-Publication Data

Czech, Jan M.
  The rhino / Jan M. Czech.
    p. cm. — (Endangered and threatened animals)
  "A MyReportLinks.com Book."
  Includes bibliographical references (p.) and index.
  ISBN 0-7660-5062-9
  1. Rhinoceroses—Juvenile literature. 2. Endangered species—Juvenile literature. I. Title. II.
Series.
  QL737.U63C92 2005
  599.66'8—dc22

                                         2004009593

Printed in the United States of America

10 9 8 7 6 5 4 3 2 1

To Our Readers:
Through the purchase of this book, you and your library gain access to the Report Links that
specifically back up this book.
The Publisher will provide access to the Report Links that back up this book and will keep these Report
Links up to date on **www.myreportlinks.com** for five years from the book's first publication date.
We have done our best to make sure all Internet addresses in this book were active and appropriate
when we went to press. However, the author and the Publisher have no control over, and assume
no liability for, the material available on those Internet sites or on other Web sites they may link to.
The usage of the MyReportLinks.com Books Web site is subject to the terms and conditions stated
on the Usage Policy Statement on **www.myreportlinks.com**.
A password may be required to access the Report Links that back up this book. The password is
found on the bottom of page 4 of this book.
Any comments or suggestions can be sent by e-mail to comments@myreportlinks.com or to the
address on the back cover.

Photo Credits: © 2002–2004 Wildlife Conservation Network, Inc., p. 42; © Cincinnati
Zoo and Botanical Garden, p. 26; © Corel Corporation, pp. 1, 3, 17, 19, 21, 23, 31, 33,
35, 38, 40; © Discovery Communications, Inc., p. 11; © International Rhino Foundation,
pp. 13, 36; © Singapore Zoological Gardens, p. 24; AP/Wide World Photos, p. 27; © Art
Explosion/Nova Development Corporation, p. 10; Enslow Publishers, Inc., p. 29; John
Bavaro, p. 15; MyReportLinks.com Books, p. 4; U.S. Fish and Wildlife Service, p. 44.

Cover Photo: Young white rhino and mother, © Digital Vision.

Contents

MyReportLinks.com Books
Great Books, Great Links, Great for Research!

The Internet sites listed on the next five pages can save you hours of research time. These Internet sites—we call them "Report Links"—are constantly changing, but we keep them up to date on our Web site.

Give it a try! Type http://www.myreportlinks.com into your browser, click on the series title, then the book title, and scroll down to the Report Links listed for this book.

The Report Links will bring you to great source documents, photographs, and illustrations. MyReportLinks.com Books save you time, feature Report Links that are kept up to date, and make report writing easier than ever!

Please see "To Our Readers" on the copyright page for important information about this book, the MyReportLinks.com Web site, and the Report Links that back up this book.

Please enter **ERH1548** if asked for a password.

Report Links

The Internet sites described below can be accessed at
http://www.myreportlinks.com

*EDITOR'S CHOICE

▶ **International Rhino Foundation**

The IRF is working to protect and conserve the five remaining rhinoceros species on earth. This organization's Web site provides a great deal of information about each species and efforts to protect them.

Link to this Internet site from http://www.myreportlinks.com

*EDITOR'S CHOICE

▶ **Black Rhinoceros**

Ninety percent of the black rhinos living in East Africa were slaughtered in the 1970s, bringing their numbers down to 2,500 from 65,000. Learn about dehorning, breeding programs, trade regulations, and why these animals are exploited.

Link to this Internet site from http://www.myreportlinks.com

*EDITOR'S CHOICE

▶ **White Rhinoceros**

Despite its name, the white rhinoceros is actually gray. Learn about the white rhino's behavior, habitat, and more at this Web site from Botswana's Department of Tourism.

Link to this Internet site from http://www.myreportlinks.com

*EDITOR'S CHOICE

▶ **Family Rhinocerotidae**

Two species of rhinoceros live in Africa while the other three live in Asia. Despite this and other differences, all rhinos share certain similarities. Learn more about rhinos at this Web site.

Link to this Internet site from http://www.myreportlinks.com

*EDITOR'S CHOICE

▶ **African Wildlife Foundation: Rhinoceros**

The rhinoceros has roamed the planet for millions of years but is currently facing extinction. Five species, numbering less than twenty thousand, are all that remain of the more than one million that once roamed the earth. Learn more about rhinos on this site.

Link to this Internet site from http://www.myreportlinks.com

*EDITOR'S CHOICE

▶ **World Wildlife Fund: Rhinos**

Rhinos are one of the largest free-roaming mammals on the planet and are an important part of their ecosystems. Read more about these animals from the World Wildlife Fund Web site.

Link to this Internet site from http://www.myreportlinks.com

 The Internet sites described below can be accessed at
http://www.myreportlinks.com

▶ **Animal Info—Sumatran Rhinoceros**
The Sumatran rhinoceros is a nocturnal herbivore that also eats some fruit, including figs, and likes to lick salt. On this Web site, learn more about where this species is currently found, population estimates, and its biology and ecology.

Link to this Internet site from http://www.myreportlinks.com

▶ **Black Rhinoceros**
The black rhino was originally found over most of Africa, south of the Sahara, but currently lives only in small pockets of the continent. Read more about this species on this Web site.

Link to this Internet site from http://www.myreportlinks.com

▶ **Cincinnati Zoo and Botanical Garden**
The Cincinnati Zoo made history when two of its Sumatran rhinos successfully mated not once, but twice. At the zoo's site, read about the historic birth of Suci on July 30, 2004.

Link to this Internet site from http://www.myreportlinks.com

▶ **Endangered Species Information, U.S. Fish & Wildlife Service**
The United States Fish and Wildlife Service lists threatened and endangered animals and plants worldwide. This USFWS page offers links to the database in which those species, including the rhinos, are listed.

Link to this Internet site from http://www.myreportlinks.com

▶ **Grass-eating Giants**
Rhinos are herbivores that graze on grass and other plant materials, including leaves and twigs. All rhinos are critically endangered. Follow the links on this site for specific information on the rhinos of Asia and Africa.

Link to this Internet site from http://www.myreportlinks.com

▶ **Houston Zoo**
This site from the Houston Zoo offers information on each rhino species. It also provides links to sites that describe some of the conservation efforts that are under way to save rhinos.

Link to this Internet site from http://www.myreportlinks.com

Any comments? Contact us: **comments@myreportlinks.com**

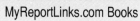

Report Links

 The Internet sites described below can be accessed at
http://www.myreportlinks.com

▶ **Indian Rhino**
The Indian rhino is a little safer from extinction than a few decades ago.
Although the animal is largely protected from poachers, Indian rhinos are
still vulnerable. Follow the links at the bottom under "Natural History"
for more information.

    Link to this Internet site from http://www.myreportlinks.com

▶ **Indian Rhinoceros**
The Indian rhino is a solitary animal, spending long hours in the water
and mud. Learn more about this species of rhino at this Web site.

    Link to this Internet site from http://www.myreportlinks.com

▶ **Indricotherium**
The Indricotherium, an ancestor of the rhino, is now extinct, but it was
one of the largest land mammals that ever existed. This hornless, three-
toed, long-legged herbivore ate leaves and twigs from the tops of trees.
View an image of this creature at this Discovery.com site.

    Link to this Internet site from http://www.myreportlinks.com

▶ **Introducing the Running Fortresses**
Once quite numerous, rhinos have drastically declined because their horns
are used in traditional Asian medicines and for the handle of Yemeni
daggers. Read about what has helped rhinos from becoming extinct.

    Link to this Internet site from http://www.myreportlinks.com

▶ **Javan Rhinoceros**
The Javan rhinoceros is critically endangered. At this site, learn more
about where this species is currently found, population estimates,
and its biology and ecology.

    Link to this Internet site from http://www.myreportlinks.com

▶ **Rhino Horn Import Ban (RHINO)**
Selling rhino horn is a lucrative business, with prices soaring to tens of
thousands of dollars for a couple of pounds. Learn more about rhinos and
the illegal trade in rhino horns.

    Link to this Internet site from http://www.myreportlinks.com

The Internet sites described below can be accessed at
http://www.myreportlinks.com

▶ Rhinoceros
This site offers information on all five species of rhinos, including habitat, range, physical characteristics, life span, and age at maturity, among other facts.

Link to this Internet site from http://www.myreportlinks.com

▶ Rhinoceros (Rhinocerotidae)
This short article provides information on the size, numbers, life span, range, habitat, food, behavior, threats, offspring, and protection status of the rhino species.

Link to this Internet site from http://www.myreportlinks.com

▶ Save the Rhino International
Numbers of all rhino populations are low and continue to decrease. At this site, learn why rhinos are threatened and what programs this international organization is funding to help save these mammals.

Link to this Internet site from http://www.myreportlinks.com

▶ Singapore Zoological Gardens
Loss of habitat and poaching for their horns and other body parts have endangered all species of rhinoceros. This Singapore Zoo site offers fact files on the five rhino species.

Link to this Internet site from http://www.myreportlinks.com

▶ SOS Rhino
This nonprofit organization works with countries around the world to raise educational awareness of the plight of rhinos and funds a wide variety of conservation efforts. Lots of information and pictures of rhinos are available.

Link to this Internet site from http://www.myreportlinks.com

▶ South African Wildlife: The Rhinoceros
This Web site from South Africa Venues provides a brief overview of the black rhino and the white rhino, both of which are found in Africa. Information on size, habitat, diet, life span, predators, and more can be found here.

Link to this Internet site from http://www.myreportlinks.com

Report Links

The Internet sites described below can be accessed at
http://www.myreportlinks.com

▶Sumatran Rhino Conservation Project
Rhino Protection Units (RPUs) are antipoaching teams that patrol areas
frequented by the Sumatran rhino. Learn more about the Sumatran Rhino
Conservation Project and what other steps are being taken to help protect
this species.

Link to this Internet site from http://www.myreportlinks.com

▶Sumatran Rhinoceros
The Sumatran rhino has had a 50 percent drop in population over the
past ten years due to poaching. This has made it the most endangered of
all the rhino species even though the Javan rhino is rarer. Read more
about this disappearing animal on the Save the Rhino Web site.

Link to this Internet site from http://www.myreportlinks.com

▶TRAFFIC
TRAFFIC is an organization that monitors the international trade of
wildlife. It also supports the conservation of wild plants, undertakes
research, and promotes enforcement of laws to protect animals and plants
from illegal trade.

Link to this Internet site from http://www.myreportlinks.com

▶What Exactly Does *Endangered* Mean?
Learn what it means when an animal is designated *endangered*. Different
organizations use different terms and labels. Familiarize yourself with the
most often-used ones.

Link to this Internet site from http://www.myreportlinks.com

▶Wildlife Authorities Take Rhino Poaching by the Horns
Scientists are using mitochondrial DNA testing and other techniques on
confiscated rhino horn to determine where the animal came from. Learn
how these methods can help save more rhinos.

Link to this Internet site from http://www.myreportlinks.com

▶World Animal Day—UN
At this site from the United Nations, learn about the United Nations
Environment Programme, which administers CITES, and its efforts to
save endangered species, including rhinos.

Link to this Internet site from http://www.myreportlinks.com

Scientific Names

There are five species of rhinoceros and eleven subspecies.

- **Black Rhino** *Diceros bicornis*
- **White Rhino** *Ceratotherium simum*
- **Indian Rhino** *Rhinoceros unicornis*
- **Javan Rhino** *Rhinoceros sondaicus*
- **Sumatran Rhino** *Dicerorhinus sumatrensis*

Average Height

4 to 6 feet (1.2 to 1.8 meters) to the shoulder

Average Weight

The five species of rhinos range from 750 pounds to 8,000 pounds (340 kilograms to 3,629 kilograms).

Life Span

In the wild, up to thirty-five years; in captivity, forty years or longer

Status

Endangered

Skin Color

Gray or brown

Teeth

Rhinos have between twenty-four and thirty-four teeth depending on the species.

Breeding Season

No particular season

Gestation Period

Varies by species but averages sixteen months

Range

Black rhinos and white rhinos are found in Africa; Javan, Indian, and Sumatran rhinos are found in Asia.

Maximum Speed

30 miles per hour (48 kilometers per hour)

Main Threat to Survival

Humans, who kill rhinos for their horns and destroy their habitat

An Ancient Species in Peril

The rhinoceros is one of the world's most ancient animal species. It has roamed the earth for nearly 50 million years. Until about 3 million years ago, rhinos were the most common land mammal in North America. There were once many more kinds of rhinos, including hornless rhinos, wooly rhinos, and the Indricotherium, all now extinct.

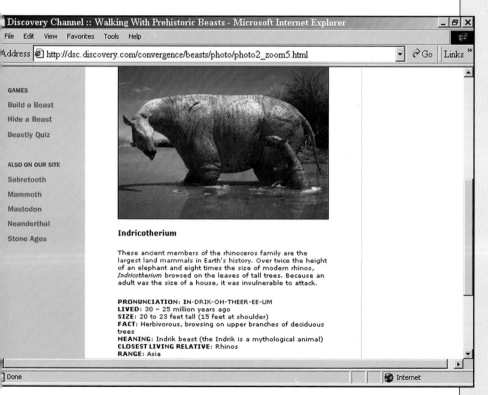

Discovery Channel :: Walking With Prehistoric Beasts - Microsoft Internet Explorer

File   Edit   View   Favorites   Tools   Help

Address http://dsc.discovery.com/convergence/beasts/photo/photo2_zoom5.html   Go   Links

GAMES

Build a Beast

Hide a Beast

Beastly Quiz

ALSO ON OUR SITE

Sabretooth

Mammoth

Mastodon

Neanderthal

Stone Ages

Indricotherium

These ancient members of the rhinoceros family are the largest land mammals in Earth's history. Over twice the height of an elephant and eight times the size of modern rhinos, *Indricotherium* browsed on the leaves of tall trees. Because an adult was the size of a house, it was invulnerable to attack.

PRONUNCIATION: IN-DRIK-OH-THEER-EE-UM
LIVED: 30 – 25 million years ago
SIZE: 20 to 23 feet tall (15 feet at shoulder)
FACT: Herbivorous, browsing on upper branches of deciduous trees
MEANING: Indrik beast (the Indrik is a mythological animal)
CLOSEST LIVING RELATIVE: Rhinos
RANGE: Asia

Done   Internet

▲ The Indricotherium was an ancient ancestor of the rhino. This giant creature stood 23 feet tall and was eight times the size of rhinos that live today.

In the case of the Indricotherium, that is probably a good thing: It was the largest land mammal in Earth's history. This giant member of the rhinoceros family stood between 18 and 23 feet (5 and 7 meters) tall, was 27 feet (8 meters) long, and weighed about 66,000 pounds (30,000 kilograms).[1] It was eight times the size of modern rhinos—as large as most houses. Other ancient rhinos looked more like horses or giraffes than their modern-day counterparts. Some scientists think that the mythical unicorn may be based on an ancient horselike one-horned rhino that actually lived.

The Indricotherium, like the dinosaur and many other ancient species, no longer exists. Its modern relatives in the rhino family face the same fate—that of becoming extinct. There are now only five species and eleven subspecies of rhino, and they are found only in Africa and Asia. How could an animal that has been around for millions of years and once was so common be in danger of disappearing from the face of the earth?

Dwindling Species

Rhinos are disappearing, unfortunately, because of us. Human beings pose the biggest threat to the rhino population through hunting and developing the lands that once made up the rhinos' habitat. According to the World Wildlife Fund, an international conservation organization, hunting and habitat destruction have reduced the rhino population by almost 90 percent since 1970.[2] Despite valiant attempts to build up and protect the rhino population, these magnificent animals are now among the most critically endangered animal species. The International Rhino Foundation (IRF), which supports and operates rhino conservation programs, reports that as of 2004, there were only about 17,470 rhinos left in the wild, with about 1,500 in captivity. According to the IRF, there are about 11,100 white rhinos, 3,610 black rhinos, 2,400 Indian rhinos, 60 Javan rhinos, and 300 Sumatran rhinos. Nearly all rhino species are on the verge of extinction.[3]

Why They Are Hunted

The word *rhinoceros* comes from the Greek *rhino,* which means "nose," and *ceros,* which means "horn." Rhino horns are made of tightly packed hair called keratin,

Northern White Rhino - Microsoft Internet Explorer

File   Edit   View   Favorites   Tools   Help

Address http://www.rhinos-irf.org/rhinoinformation/whiterhino/subspecies/northern.htm   Go   Links

Rhino Information
IRF Programs
What is the IRF?
Education
How You Can Horn In
Technical Programs

ADOPT A RHINO

White Rhino   Southern   Northern

Northern White Rhino

Ceratotherium simum cottoni

Dvur Kralove

The Northern White Rhino is critically endangered in ironic contrast to the status of its relative the Southern White Rhino, which is the most abundant of all rhino taxa known today. Once ranging in large numbers throughout north-central Africa south of the Sahara, wild Northern White Rhino populations have been again reduced to only about 15 individuals located in Garamba National Park, Democratic Republic of the Congo (DRC). There has been much concern about the status of this last surviving population because of the recent civil wars and attendant disruptions.

Done   Internet

▲ *Rhino horns are extremely valuable in certain parts of the world. Poachers from Sudan, a country in Africa, have killed and are continuing to kill northern white rhinos at an alarming rate because they can sell the horn for about $2,500 per pound.*

which is like human hair and nails. Rhinos use their horns to defend themselves against other animals. Unfortunately, it is for their horns that people hunt rhinos, because those horns are highly valued in certain cultures and fetch a huge amount of money.

Poachers, people who take or kill wild animals illegally, hunt rhinos on wildlife refuges, places where they are supposed to be protected. Rhinos are also hunted in the wild, in their natural habitats. Rhinos often die very slowly after being shot with guns or arrows. Many times, their horns are taken while they are still alive.

Although it is illegal to trade in rhino horn because the rhino is endangered, the market is a booming one that reaches around the world. In Yemen, an Asian country at the southern tip of the Arabian peninsula, rhino horn is used to make handles for knives called jambiyas. Jambiyas are considered precious and, in many families, are handed down from generation to generation. In eastern Asia, rhinoceros horns are ground up and used in medicines. The rhino horn is the most important part of the rhino to hunters, but rhino nails, hooves, blood, urine, and hide are also traded and used in medicines.

Efforts are under way to protect this ancient animal, but time and tradition are both against the rhino. And humans, who pose the greatest threat to the rhino's survival, are the only ones who can now save it.

Vegetarian Giants

Rhinos, like humans, are mammals. And like humans, they are warm-blooded and have backbones and hair. Female rhinos give birth to live babies and nurse their young just as human females do.

But unlike humans, rhinos have hooves like horses and are part of the same order. They have only three toes on each hoof. A rhino's skin is different from one species to the next but is between half an inch to three quarters of an inch

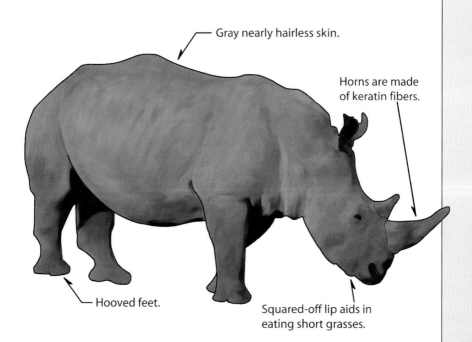

Gray nearly hairless skin.

Horns are made of keratin fibers.

Hooved feet.

Squared-off lip aids in eating short grasses.

▲ A southern white rhino, now the least endangered of the rhinos.

thick. That is about as thick as the length of your little finger. And unlike many people, rhinos are herbivores—they eat only plants. They are either grazers, feeding mostly on grasses, or browsers, eating the leaves and branches of trees. Their lips have adapted over time to make it easier for them to graze and browse for food. Rhinos have between twenty-four and thirty-four teeth, including twelve to fourteen pairs of molars that are not sharp and are used for grinding.

▶ Breeding Habits

Rhinos are not able to reproduce quickly, which also plays a part in their shrinking numbers. The rhino's gestation period, or the length of time a mother carries her young until it is born, is about sixteen months. Secondly, the male rhino, known as a bull, is not able to father a baby rhino, or calf, until the male is about twelve years old. There is also no set time of the year that rhinos breed or give birth. Breeding can take place any time of the year that the female, or cow, is in estrus, the period during which she can become pregnant. Female rhinos are able to reproduce at around age six and have a calf once every two or three years after that.

Even though a rhino calf nurses for about two years, it begins to eat plants when it is only a week old. While it nurses, the rhino calf is kept hidden and protected by its mother until it is strong enough to venture out on its own. While adult rhinos have no predators apart from humans, baby rhinos are in danger of being attacked by lions, hyenas, crocodiles, and tigers.

▶ Home, Sweet Home

Rhinos live in the wild, in reserves, in private parks, and in captivity in zoos. Their natural habitat ranges from open grasslands called savannas to dense forests. Because rhinos like to drink water every day, their habitat must include a watering spot where they can not only drink but also wallow in the water and mud to cool themselves off. Rhinos can go for up to four days without water, but it is a hardship for them to do so.

▶ Gentle Giants?

All rhino species have a reputation for being aggressive. It is said that the black rhino will charge anything that moves. But rhinos are also easily frightened, and because

▲ Tick birds rest on the back of a black rhino. The rhino offers these birds a lookout place from which to find food while the birds eat parasites on the rhino's skin. These birds also warn the rhino when trouble approaches.

their eyesight is poor, they may attack because they think an enemy is approaching. Rhinos have highly developed senses of smell and hearing and depend on these two senses much more than their eyesight.

They are especially gentle when it comes to birds hitching a ride. In Africa, cattle egrets can often be found riding on the backs of rhinoceroses and other large mammals. From their perch, they have a good view of the grasshoppers and other creatures that crawl on the ground.[1] Egrets help the rhino by eating many of the bugs that live on the rhino's skin. They can also act as an early warning. If an egret sees something approaching, it will take flight, and that warns the rhino to be on the lookout.

The Five Rhino Species

There are currently five species of rhino remaining in the world. The black rhino and the white rhino are native to Africa, although neither name adequately describes the animal's skin color, which is mostly gray. The Indian rhino, Javan rhino, and Sumatran rhino live in Asia.

The White Rhino

After the elephant, the white rhino is the largest land animal on earth. White rhinos can weigh up to 8,000 pounds (3,628 kilograms) and stand 6 feet (1.8 meters) tall. Their name comes from the Afrikaans language spoken in South Africa. Early British settlers there misinterpreted the word *weit* as *white*.[2] *Weit*, which means "wide," was used to describe the rhino's mouth.

The white rhino has two horns, one behind the other. It also has a wide, square lip and is a grazer, feeding mainly on grass. The white rhino's head is larger and heavier than the heads of the other rhino species. And because the

▲ Although the Indian rhino is about half a foot taller than the white rhino, above, the white rhino is about two and a half feet longer than the Indian rhino. Both rhinos weigh about the same—between 4,000 and 6,000 pounds.

white rhino grazes for food, the muscles in its neck are quite developed so that it can lift its enormous head.

The International Rhino Foundation estimates that there are about 11,100 white rhinos left in Africa. This population has increased from a low of forty animals in 1900. White rhinos are less endangered than the other four rhino species.

But there are two subspecies of white rhino, and their status differs greatly. The southern white rhino was the first rhino species to come close to extinction, but conservation efforts have boosted its population so that it is now the least endangered rhino. Protected on farms and reserves mainly in South Africa, its population is growing.

The northern white rhino, on the other hand, is critically endangered. Its range used to include much of central Africa. Its habitat today is limited to the Garamba National Park in the Democratic Republic of Congo, formerly known as Zaire. Although this is a place where the rhinos are supposed to receive protection, their numbers have been cut in half by heavily-armed poachers over a fourteen-month period from April 2003 to June 2004. As of July 2004, when aerial surveys were taken of the park, there were only between 17 and 22 animals left in this, their last refuge.[3] Another ten northern white rhinos live in captivity in zoos in the Czech Republic and the United States. Despite efforts to save them, it is very possible that the northern white rhino will go extinct.

The Black Rhino

The black rhino, whose name may have come from the dark soils it wallows around in, also has two horns. It is smaller than the white rhino, weighing up to 3,000 pounds (1,360 kilograms) and standing between 4.5 and 5.5 feet (1.4 and 1.7 meters) tall. The black rhino has especially pointed prehensile lips that help it to grasp the food it browses for. Both black rhinos and white rhinos have skin that hangs in folds and looks like leather, with lots of knobby parts, but it is actually quite smooth and soft to the touch.

Black rhinos once ranged across much of Africa but are now found in small areas in southern and eastern Africa. The black rhino population is estimated to be at 3,610, down from 65,000 in 1970.

The Indian Rhino

The Indian rhino, so-called because it once lived throughout India, now lives on eight reserves in India and Nepal.

In 1970, there were approximately 65,000 black rhinos in Africa. By 1992, the population had dwindled down to 2,300. Efforts to stop poaching have allowed this species to make a small recovery. Now about 3,610 black rhinos can be found in the wild.

It can weigh up to 6,000 pounds (2,721 kilograms) and stand about 6 feet (2 meters) tall. It is the third largest land mammal, smaller only than the white rhino and the elephant. Unlike the smooth skin of the African rhinos, the most conspicuous characteristic of the Indian rhino is the deep folds in its skin. The Indian rhino, mainly a grazer, differs from African rhinos in another way: It has only one horn.

There are about 2,400 Indian rhinos left, and theirs is a real success story. Early in the twentieth century, there were only about two hundred Indian rhinos remaining. Over the years, wildlife authorities in India and Nepal

have worked to protect the Indian rhino from hunters and poachers, allowing the rhino population a chance to grow.

▷ The Javan Rhino

The Javan rhino is the rarest of the five rhino species and also one of the most endangered, since only about 60 remain. Javan rhinos live only in two national parks: one in Java, an island that is part of Indonesia, and another in Vietnam. Javan rhinos weigh between 2,000 and 5,000 pounds (907 and 2,268 kilograms) and stand about 5 feet (1.5 meters) tall. The Javan rhino has one horn and skin plates like the Indian rhino but is much smaller.

As recently as thirty years ago, many scientists thought the Javan rhino was extinct, especially in Vietnam because they were almost never seen there. People living near their habitat claimed to see them, but there was no real proof until scientists were able to set camera traps and get pictures of the shy rhino.

The Javan rhino used to have a range that included India, Bangladesh, China, Myanmar, Thailand, Laos, Cambodia, Vietnam, Malaysia, and Indonesia. The species lost much of its jungle habitat during the Vietnam War. Agent Orange, a chemical agent for killing plants, was used during the war to cut down jungle growth, but it also destroyed the trees from which the rhino fed. There is some good news about the Javan rhino, though. Four calves have been born in the last four years, and these are believed to be the first births in many years. They may be the beginning of an upturn in the Javan rhino population.

▷ The Sumatran Rhino

The Sumatran rhino lives in Sumatra, an island that is part of Indonesia, and Malaysia. The Sumatran rhino is

▲ *Like other rhinos, the Indian rhino is generally a solitary animal. It spends long periods of time lying in water and wallowing in mud.*

considered to be the most endangered rhino species. The Sumatran rhino population has decreased 50 percent over the last fifteen years mainly because of hunters. Fewer than three hundred Sumatran rhinos are alive today, and that number is shrinking because they are hunted and not well protected.

Sumatran rhinos weigh between 1,300 and 2,000 pounds (590 and 907 kilograms) and stand from 3 to 5 feet (under 1 meter to 1.5 meters) tall. Like their African cousins, they have two horns. The Sumatran rhino is the only rhino species to have long hair, which is thickest when the rhino is young.[4] Sumatran rhinos are also the only rhinos to have sharp canine teeth on their lower jaw. These teeth are used for fighting.

The Sumatran rhino prefers to live in the dense forest areas of Sumatra, Myanmar, Malaysia, and Thailand. As the human population in these areas increases, the Sumatran rhino's habitat grows smaller and smaller. Another blow to the Sumatran rhino's population occurred in 2003 when all seven of the Sumatran rhinos in the Sumatra Rhino Sanctuary at Sungai Dusun in Malaysia died. Their deaths were due to infection that was probably caused by a parasite. The same parasite causes sleeping sickness in humans.

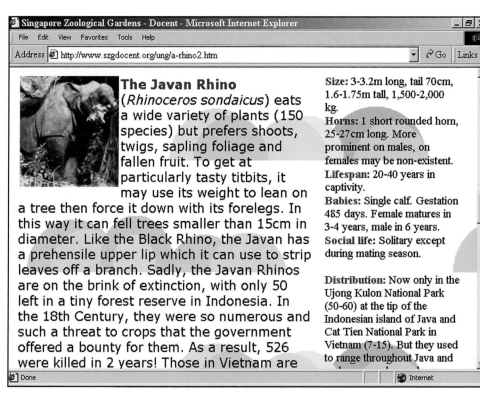

Singapore Zoological Gardens - Docent - Microsoft Internet Explorer

File   Edit   View   Favorites   Tools   Help

Address http://www.szgdocent.org/ung/a-rhino2.htm   Go   Links

The Javan Rhino (*Rhinoceros sondaicus*) eats a wide variety of plants (150 species) but prefers shoots, twigs, sapling foliage and fallen fruit. To get at particularly tasty titbits, it may use its weight to lean on a tree then force it down with its forelegs. In this way it can fell trees smaller than 15cm in diameter. Like the Black Rhino, the Javan has a prehensile upper lip which it can use to strip leaves off a branch. Sadly, the Javan Rhinos are on the brink of extinction, with only 50 left in a tiny forest reserve in Indonesia. In the 18th Century, they were so numerous and such a threat to crops that the government offered a bounty for them. As a result, 526 were killed in 2 years! Those in Vietnam are

Size: 3-3.2m long, tail 70cm, 1.6-1.75m tall, 1,500-2,000 kg.
Horns: 1 short rounded horn, 25-27cm long. More prominent on males, on females may be non-existent.
Lifespan: 20-40 years in captivity.
Babies: Single calf. Gestation 485 days. Female matures in 3-4 years, male in 6 years.
Social life: Solitary except during mating season.

Distribution: Now only in the Ujong Kulon National Park (50-60) at the tip of the Indonesian island of Java and Cat Tien National Park in Vietnam (7-15). But they used to range throughout Java and

Done   Internet

▲ *The Javan rhino is also known as the Asian Lesser One-Horned Rhino. The Indian rhino is also referred to as the Asian Greater One-Horned Rhino. The Javan rhino is considered "lesser" because it is smaller than the Indian rhino.*

▶ Rhinos in Captivity

Rhinos can be found in captivity all over the world. Captive rhinos, moved from the wild in a process called translocation, live mainly in zoos and rhino sanctuaries. These sanctuaries can be publicly funded or paid for by private citizens. Rhinos are kept in captivity in an effort to protect them from poachers and to keep them from becoming extinct. Many sanctuaries are surrounded by electric fences to keep poachers out, and they are patrolled by guards who are armed.

Most zoos and sanctuaries have captive breeding programs to try to keep rhino populations growing. Some breeding programs are very successful while others are not, and they are not without controversy. For example, the Sumatran Rhino Trust was formed, according to the group itself, to "catch enough breeding pairs of rhinos in the wild to start a viable population in captivity and thereby stem the slide toward extinction."[5] Rhino pairs were placed in zoos in the United States. The project was very expensive, and the World Wildlife Fund, for one, objected to the program, saying that the money could have been better spent keeping the rhinos in a sanctuary in their natural habitat rather than in zoos. They may have been correct. Seven animals were placed in zoos, and soon after placement, four had died.

But there have been successes. In 2001, at the Cincinnati Zoo, a Sumatran rhino named Emi gave birth to a calf named Andalas, the first Sumatran rhino to be born and bred in captivity in 112 years.[6] On July 30, 2004, Emi gave birth to a second calf, this time a female, named Suci (an Indonesian word meaning "sacred"). With that birth, Emi became the first Sumatran rhino in history to produce two rhino calves in captivity.

Back   Forward   Stop   Review   Home   Explore   Favorites   History

Untitled Document - Microsoft Internet Explorer

File   Edit   View   Favorites   Tools   Help

Address nnatizoo.org/Conservation/GlobalConservation/SumatranRhino/SumatranFilmstrip/filmstrip6.html   Go   Links

Sumatran rhino calf

Done   Internet

Suci, a female Sumatran rhino calf, made a historic entrance into the world on July 30, 2004, at the Cincinnati Zoo. With Suci's birth, her mother, Emi, became the first Sumatran rhino to give birth to two calves in captivity.

The zoo's vice president of Animal Sciences, Dr. Terry Roth, characterized the historic birth this way: "Because Sumatran rhinos are on the brink of extinction, this calf serves as a lifeline for a species clinging desperately to survival."[7] And in August 2004, a black rhinoceros calf named Ajubu was born to Lembe, a first-time mother, at the San Diego Zoo's Wild Animal Park. The park has had ten black rhino births to date, helping the critically endangered species to survive.

Chapter 3 ▶

The Rhino's Only Predator

With its fearsome size and horn, the adult rhino has only one predator: man. Humans have managed through hunting the rhino and through destroying its natural habitat to come close to wiping it off the face of the earth entirely.

▷ Poaching

Although international trading in rhino horns has been illegal since 1977, the practice is still a booming black-market

▲ Indian forest officials collect wires that were used by poachers to electrocute two rhinos in the Pabitora Wildlife Sanctuary before taking their horns.

business. Poaching is the biggest threat to all rhino species. Because rhino horn and other body parts are used in traditional medicines in China and other countries in Asia, there is a thriving market for them, and buyers are willing to pay large amounts of money for them.

▶ The Demand for Rhino Horn

Poachers hunt rhinos illegally on reserves and in their natural habitats. Most are men who live in some of the poorest countries in the world. If it were not for poaching, they would ordinarily make very little money. One rhino horn might bring them more than a year's wages earned legally. But poachers are not the only ones who kill rhinos. Wealthy sport hunters are also to blame. According to Dr. Harrison Kojwang, the regional representative for the World Wildlife Fund in Southern Africa, "Prompt action is required by the South African and Zimbabwean authorities to . . . clamp down on the cross-border hunting forays by readily identifiable hunting parties."[1]

Poachers are usually well equipped with weapons provided for them by the people who hire them to kill rhinos and deliver their horns. Poachers and park rangers are at war with each other over the rhino and other endangered species that live in the closely guarded game reserves. Park rangers in reserves are under orders to shoot poachers on sight. Poachers, park rangers, and others have lost their lives in the battle over rhinos.

Poachers kill rhinos with guns, spears, traps dug in the ground, and through electrocution when they can find an electrical line in the rhino habitat to cut down and lay across the rhino's path. Once the rhino is downed, the poachers saw off the horns and the hooves. Often, the rhino is still alive during this and dies later from its wounds.

Loss of Habitat

While poaching is by far the biggest threat to the rhino, loss of habitat also plays a significant role. As human populations grow, more land is needed to support it. This often results in pushing wild animals farther and farther

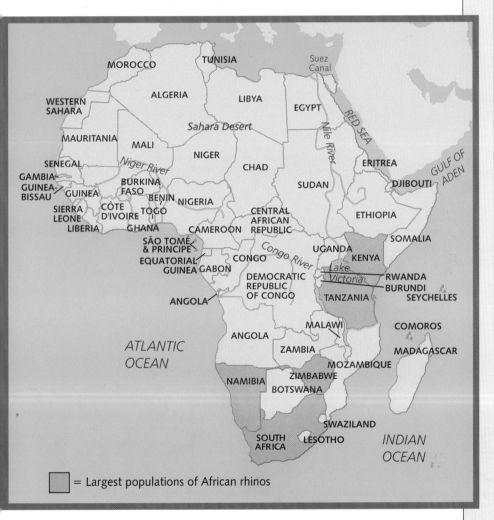

= Largest populations of African rhinos

▲ The black rhino and the white rhino are the two rhino species that are native to Africa. Once widespread throughout the continent, African rhinos are now found mostly in the grasslands and tropical bushlands of five countries: Namibia, South Africa, Zimbabwe, Tanzania, and Kenya.

into their wild habitat, which often creates a compacted population. Rhinos, as grazers and browsers, require a large territory in which to roam and find food. Logging; land being cleared for large farms that produce oil palm, wood pulp, coffee, rubber, cashews, and cocoa; and people looking for land on which to settle all force rhinos into smaller and smaller habitats.

But the rhino has also been forced to share its habitat with people for other reasons. Civil wars that have raged on for decades in some African and Asian countries have forced many people from their homes. Some of those refugees have sought refuge in wildlife sanctuaries. Once there, the human population takes natural resources, such as water and trees, which they use for firewood and shelter, that the wild animals, including rhinos, also need to survive.

As humans move into rhino territory, more and more habitat is destroyed. Not only are trees disappearing in some rhino habitats, but grass is also disappearing. Traditional nomadic herding practices that moved cattle to new pastures and avoided overgrazing have changed. Now, due to economic and population demands, cattle are raised in just one place, which has a devastating effect on the savanna's ecosystem.[2] Cattle are grazers just as some rhinos are, and as they eat the rhinos' food supply, rhinos are forced to look elsewhere. As ecosystems are destroyed, so is the rhino population.

Chapter 4

The Growing Concern for the Rhino's Welfare

At the turn of the twentieth century, there were nearly one million rhinos living in Asia and Africa. By the dawn of the twenty-first century, only about sixteen thousand remained. The five species of rhinos left in the world are all considered endangered by the United States Fish and Wildlife Service's Threatened and Endangered Species System List. That list includes plant and animal species worldwide that are threatened and endangered.

▲ Two black rhinos greet each other. Despite the name, black rhinos are actually dark gray and usually hairless, but they may have short, coarse stubble. Black rhinos are also known for eating many plants that are poisonous to other animals.

The International Union for the Conservation of Nature and Natural Resources (IUCN), also known as the World Conservation Union, is a worldwide organization made up of many groups who volunteer their services and expertise to try to save endangered species, including the rhino. The IUCN has placed the Sumatran, Javan, and black rhino species on its critically endangered list, which is known as the Red List of Threatened Species.

The concern for the dwindling number of rhinos left in the world is widespread and includes conservation organizations, private citizens, zoos, and national and state governments. While some progress has been made in protecting the rhinos and introducing breeding programs to help ensure that populations will not simply vanish, it is still a race against time, poachers, and the loss of habitat to save the rhino.

Rhino Horn Trade

Rhino horns can bring up to $2,600 a pound on the black market. For centuries, the Chinese have used rhino horn in medicines, believing that it reduces fever, among other things. Some studies done by researchers at a university in Hong Kong have shown that rhino horn does reduce fever in rats. But researchers have also found that Chinese traditional medicines containing the horns of water buffalo, which are not endangered, also work to reduce fevers.[1] Belief and practice forged over many years is not easily changed, however.

The World Wildlife Fund and the IUCN jointly monitor trade in wild plants and animals to ensure that it does not pose a threat to the conservation of nature. Their monitoring includes tracking the sale and distribution of rhino horn through the Trade Records Analysis of Flora and Fauna in Commerce, or TRAFFIC. Agents who work for TRAFFIC pretend to be buyers and collectors who are looking for information on prices and the availability of animal parts, like rhino horns, that are sold illegally. Despite laws that ban the trade of rhino horn, it is still a very profitable business throughout much of the world.

▷ What Can Be Done?

Since rhino horn has been used in traditional Chinese medicines for centuries, its demand will probably not decrease before the rhino becomes extinct. Laws banning the trade in rhino horn seem to have had little effect. There are, however, programs sponsored by conservation organizations that are looking into substitutes, such as water buffalo horn, for rhino horn.

　　Jambiyas, the decorative daggers prized by wealthy Yemenis, account for the second largest use of rhino horn. Because of their rhino horn handles, they are prized and passed down for generations to young men as a symbol of masculinity.

For the most part, rhinos avoid ▷ human beings. If threatened, however, rhinos will charge people, and mothers with calves will charge whether provoked or not.

The trade in black rhino horn that is used to make dagger handles is largely responsible for the decline of the black rhino population, but things are looking up. In the mid-1980s, some conservationists were able to convince the government of Yemen to drastically reduce the rhino horn trade to that country. The plan included encouraging the use of water buffalo horn for dagger handles as well as not allowing dagger makers to be relicensed if they were caught using rhino horn.

Education: The Key to Saving Rhinos

Letting people know about the effects of the rhino horn trade on the worldwide rhino population is one way to help ensure the rhino's survival. Conservation groups and zoo programs hope to raise awareness that the world is dangerously close to losing several if not all rhino species. To that end, the United States Fish and Wildlife Service began a program in the United States aimed at educating Asian immigrants, who were most likely to use traditional Chinese medicines containing rhino horn, about just how few rhinos are left in the wild.

The United States Fish and Wildlife Service along with the Convention on International Trade in Endangered Species of Wild Fauna and Flora, or CITES, also passed the Rhinoceros and Tiger Conservation Act of 1994. As stated in the law, its purpose is "to assist in the conservation of rhinoceros and tigers by supporting the conservation programs of nations whose activities directly or indirectly affect rhinoceros and tiger populations."[2] The law also includes resolutions that prohibit the trade of endangered wildlife species and provide money for ongoing conservation efforts.

▲ *There will be fewer scenes like this, of rhinos in the wild, if the illegal trade in rhino horn continues.*

Money talks in other ways. The government of the United States monitors countries that are involved in the illegal trade of endangered animals. If those countries do not seem to be adhering to the laws protecting endangered animals, they can and have been fined large amounts of money.

▷ Dehorning

Another attempt to halt the trade in rhino horn and save the rhino from extinction is a practice called dehorning. The thought behind this practice is that a rhino without

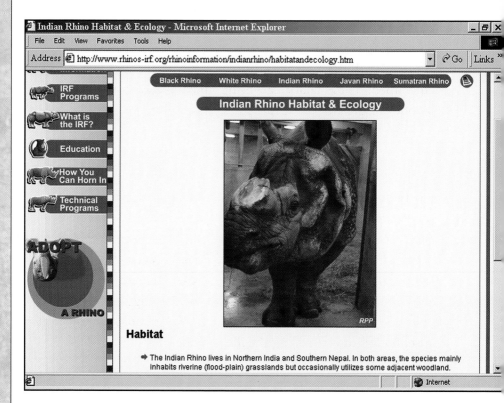

Black Rhino   White Rhino   Indian Rhino   Javan Rhino   Sumatran Rhino

Indian Rhino Habitat & Ecology

IRF Programs

What is the IRF?

Education

How You Can Horn In

Technical Programs

ADOPT A RHINO

RPP

Habitat

➡ The Indian Rhino lives in Northern India and Southern Nepal. In both areas, the species mainly inhabits riverine (flood-plain) grasslands but occasionally utilizes some adjacent woodland.

This rhino has been dehorned in hopes of making it less appealing to poachers. Its horn, made of the same substance that our fingernails are made of, will eventually grow back.

its horn is less attractive to poachers. When a rhino is dehorned, it is first shot with a tranquilizer dart to make it unconscious. Then a veterinarian removes the horn with a saw, leaving only a stub, which will grow back at the rate of about two inches a year.

The program is not foolproof, though, and it is very expensive. Unfortunately, poachers still sometimes kill dehorned animals to save themselves the trouble of tracking a rhino only to find it does not have its horn.

One of the added benefits of dehorning involves dehorning safaris, where hunters pay a fee to track and shoot the rhinos with tranquilizer darts before they are dehorned. These safaris can bring much-needed tourism money to the areas in Africa where rhinos live.

Horn Identification

Once a rhino is killed and its horn is removed, strategies to track the poachers and traders become important to shutting down the illegal market in horns. One way that conservationists hope to do this is through rhino horn "fingerprinting." Rhino horns reflect the habitat of the rhino since elements of local vegetation, climate, and geology are absorbed through digestion. Being able to identify where a particular horn came from could be a useful tool for controlling the illegal trade in rhino horn.

Another way to identify and track a rhino horn is by inserting a microchip into it. This is done while a rhino is unconscious, often when the rhino is being moved to a safer location.

Translocation

Translocation involves moving rhinos from wild habitats where they are easily poached to safer areas where they can be watched over and protected. National parks and conservation organizations have undertaken translocation projects in both Africa and India. The rhinos are moved to Intensive Protection Zones, or IPZs. These can be on government property or in private sanctuaries. One of the most famous translocation efforts was called Operation Rhino. It started in 1961 by redistributing white rhinos and continued into the 1970s as a means of saving the black rhino from extinction.

Translocating an enormous animal like the rhino is no easy task, but there have been breakthroughs over the years that have made the process easier. The tranquilizers used to sedate the animals have improved. Once a rhino is shot with a tranquilizer dart, it will sink to the ground. The dart is often shot from a helicopter rather than tracking the animal on the ground, which can be dangerous.

▲ *Despite their bulky appearance, rhinos are surprisingly nimble animals. They can turn quickly in small spaces, and the white rhino is able to reach speeds of 50 miles per hour.*

Helicopters are also used to transport the rhino in a special net.

Making Rhino Horn Trade Legal

The sale of rhino horn and other rhino products has been banned in 130 countries, but the ban has not stopped poaching as the value of rhino horn on the black market continues to increase. Some wildlife officials believe the way to deal with this is to lift the ban. There is a large supply of rhino horn in Africa that has been obtained through the dehorning program, and some officials feel that making that horn available legally would help end poaching. Other officials feel that if rhinos could be raised on farms, as cattle are, and then dehorned, the supply of rhino horn would satisfy the demand, and the rhino would be saved from extinction. These advocates of legalizing trade in rhino horn believe that the money from legal rhino-horn trade could then be used to fund programs that protect the rhino.

Chapter 5

The Future of Rhinos

Although rhinos have been around for millions of years, humans have brought them to the brink of extinction. Of the many rhino species that once roamed the world, only five remain. If efforts to save these species are unsuccessful, rhinos could cease to exist in our lifetime.

▲ The one-horned Indian rhino features folds of skin that look like the plates on a suit of armor.

▶ Rhino Populations

The white rhino nearly became extinct at the turn of the twentieth century. According to a Web site for the University of the Western Cape in South Africa, "The uncontrolled killing of southern white rhinos for sport or for their horns had reduced the population down to only twenty animals located in the Umfolozi Game Reserve in KwaZulu/Natal."[1] The KwaZulu/Natal Parks Board took action, and those animals were saved. By 1961, there were enough rhinos to translocate some as part of Operation Rhino. White rhino populations are still increasing, and there are over seven thousand of them living in South Africa where they are protected and breeding programs are in effect.

The black rhino has not fared as well as the white rhino. The black rhino population has dropped from about 65,000 in 1970 to about 3,610 today.[2] The black rhino has also benefited from translocation, and while its overall numbers in Africa are decreasing, the black rhino population in South Africa is growing because of conservation efforts there on the part of the government and private citizens.

Of the three species of Asian rhinos, the Indian rhino has the largest population. About 2,400 live in northern India and southern Nepal. Poaching remains a problem, but this species is fiercely protected by Indian and Nepalese wildlife authorities.

The Javan rhino population remained unchanged at around fifty for almost twenty years. Then in 2001 it was discovered that four rhinos were born in Ujung Kulon National Park in Java. The World Wildlife Fund and the national park authority in Ujung Kulon conducted a survey over eighteen months. Their results, which came from

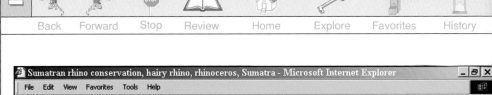

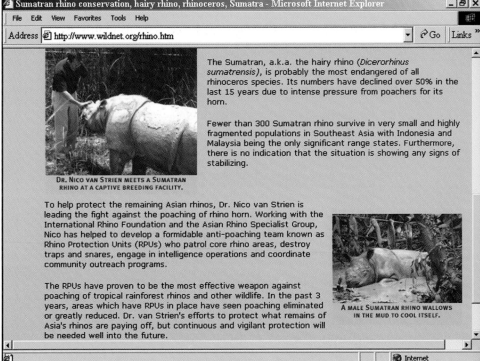

Sumatran rhino conservation, hairy rhino, rhinoceros, Sumatra - Microsoft Internet Explorer

File   Edit   View   Favorites   Tools   Help

Address   http://www.wildnet.org/rhino.htm   Go   Links

The Sumatran, a.k.a. the hairy rhino (*Dicerorhinus sumatrensis*), is probably the most endangered of all rhinoceros species. Its numbers have declined over 50% in the last 15 years due to intense pressure from poachers for its horn.

Fewer than 300 Sumatran rhino survive in very small and highly fragmented populations in Southeast Asia with Indonesia and Malaysia being the only significant range states. Furthermore, there is no indication that the situation is showing any signs of stabilizing.

DR. NICO VAN STRIEN MEETS A SUMATRAN RHINO AT A CAPTIVE BREEDING FACILITY.

To help protect the remaining Asian rhinos, Dr. Nico van Strien is leading the fight against the poaching of rhino horn. Working with the International Rhino Foundation and the Asian Rhino Specialist Group, Nico has helped to develop a formidable anti-poaching team known as Rhino Protection Units (RPUs) who patrol core rhino areas, destroy traps and snares, engage in intelligence operations and coordinate community outreach programs.

The RPUs have proven to be the most effective weapon against poaching of tropical rainforest rhinos and other wildlife. In the past 3 years, areas which have RPUs in place have seen poaching eliminated or greatly reduced. Dr. van Strien's efforts to protect what remains of Asia's rhinos are paying off, but continuous and vigilant protection will be needed well into the future.

A MALE SUMATRAN RHINO WALLOWS IN THE MUD TO COOL ITSELF.

Internet

△ While the other four rhino species are hairless or have a little stubble, the Sumatran rhino is covered in hair.

camera traps that were set in rhinoceros habitat and a DNA analysis of the animals' droppings, confirmed the four rhino births.[3]

The most seriously endangered rhino species, the Sumatran rhino, is actually greater in number than the Javan rhino. About three hundred exist today, but they are the most seriously threatened by humans. Like other rhino species, these hairy rhinos are poached for their horn and other body parts. Their habitat is shrinking each day as humans move farther into it.

Tools   Search   Notes   Discuss   Go!

The Future

There are many things being done by conservation groups to save the rhino from extinction. Captive breeding programs in zoos and rhino sanctuaries offer some hope that the rhino will not disappear from the face of the earth. The American Zoo and Aquarium Association has instituted the Species Survival Plan to encourage captive breeding programs. This program has been successful, producing more than fifty rhino births since 1995.

Not all conservationists believe that breeding programs are the answer, however. Some consider them to be last-ditch efforts to save rhinos and point out that they do not address the bigger picture of protecting habitat, stopping illegal poaching and trade in rhino parts, and returning rhinos to the wild. But the question remains, how can we return rhinos to the wild without captive breeding programs?

In March 2004, a pair of black rhino calves in South Africa was moved from a wildlife rehabilitation center to the Addo Elephant National Park in the Eastern Cape. The calves, Kapela and Thandi, had been abandoned by their mothers and raised in the rehabilitation facility. Eventually they will be released back into the wild where, it is hoped, they will breed and live long lives roaming free. Their story offers a small light at the end of a very long, dark tunnel that remains for the future of the rhino.

The Endangered and Threatened Wildlife List

This series is based on the Endangered and Threatened Wildlife list compiled by the U.S. Fish and Wildlife Service (USFWS). Each book explores an endangered or threatened animal, tells why it has become endangered or threatened, and explains the efforts being made to restore the species' population.

The United States Fish and Wildlife Service, in the Department of the Interior, and the National Marine Fisheries Service, in the Department of Commerce, share responsibility for administration of the Endangered Species Act.

In 1973, Congress took the farsighted step of creating the Endangered Species Act, widely regarded as the world's strongest and most effective wildlife conservation law. It set an ambitious goal: to reverse the alarming trend of human-caused extinction that threatened the ecosystems we all share.

The complete list of Endangered and Threatened Wildlife and Plants can be found at **http://endangered.fws.gov/wildlife.html#Species**.

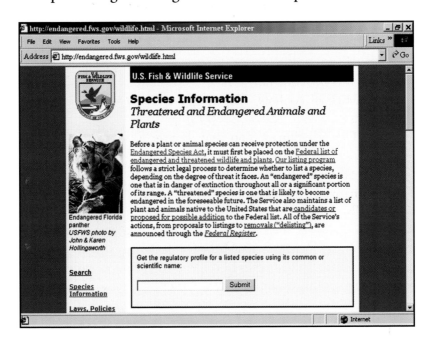

Chapter Notes

Chapter 1. An Ancient Species in Peril

1. The Columbus Zoo and Aquarium, "Pachyderms: Rhino Facts," n.d., <http://www.colszoo.org/animalareas/pacderm/rhinfact.html> (June 15, 2004).

2. The World Wildlife Fund, "Wildlife Trade," n.d., <http://worldwildlife.org/trade/> (June 10, 2004).

3. The International Rhino Foundation, "Rhino Information: The Extinction Crisis for Rhinos," n.d., <http://www.rhinos-irf.org/rhinoinformation/extinction/index.htm> (June 10, 2004).

Chapter 2. Vegetarian Giants

1. Louis and Margery Milne, *The Secret Life of Animals* (New York: Dutton, 1993), p. 177.

2. The International Rhino Foundation, "Rhino Information—White Rhino," n.d., <http://www.rhinos-irf.org/rhinoinformation/whiterhino/index.htm> (June 15, 2004).

3. BBC News, "White Rhino Numbers Are Halved," Friday, August 6, 2004, <http://news.bbc.co.uk/1/hi/sci/tech/3542060.stm> (August 8, 2004).

4. The Columbus Zoo and Aquarium, "Pachyderms: Rhino Facts," n.d., <http://www.colszoo.org/animalareas/pacderm/rhinfact.html> (June 15, 2004).

5. Michael Nichols, *Keepers of the Kingdom* (New York: Thomasson-Grant & Lickle, 1996), p. 14.

6. The Cincinnati Zoo and Botanical Garden, "It's a Girl! Cincinnati Zoo's Sumatran Rhino Makes History with Second Calf," July 30, 2004, <http://www.cincinnatizoo.org/index2.html> (August 10, 2004).

7. Ibid.

Chapter 3. The Rhino's Only Predator

1. World Wildlife Fund, *WWF Newsroom*, "Commercial poaching pressures Zimbabwe's rhinos," August 25, 2003, <http://www.panda.org/news_facts/newsroom/other_news/news.cfm?unewsID=8464> (June 10, 2004).

2. Tony Hare, *Habitats* (New York: MacMillan, 1994), p. 89.

Chapter 4. The Growing Concern for the Rhino's Welfare

1. Smithsonian National Zoological Park, Friends of the National Zoo, *Zoogoer*, Melissa Blouin, "Rhino Horns and Humans," January/February 1997, <http://natzoo.si .edu/Publications/ZooGoer/1997/1/hornsandhumans.cfm> (June 21, 2004).

2. United States Fish and Wildlife Service, International Affairs, "Public Law 103-391 [H.R. 4924], Section 3, also known as The Rhinoceros and Tiger Conservation Act of 1994," October 23, 1992, <http://international.fws.gov/ laws/rtc-fv.html> (June 14, 2004).

Chapter 5. The Future of Rhinos

1. University of the Western Cape, Botany Department, "Enviro Facts: White Rhino," n.d., <http://www.botany.uwc .ac.za/Envfacts/facts/rhinos.htm> (June 24, 2004).

2. The International Rhino Foundation, "Rhino Information—Black Rhino," n.d., <http://www.rhinos-irf .org/rhinoinformation/blackrhino/index.htm> (June 15, 2004).

3. Nick Eason, CNN.com, "Rare Javan Rhinos back from the brink," October 12, 2001, <http://www.cnn .com/2001/WORLD/asiapcf/southeast/10/12/indonesia.rhi no/> (June 10, 2004).

Further Reading

Allen, Christina. *Hippos in the Night: Autobiographical Adventures in Africa.* New York: HarperCollins, 2003.

Arnold, Caroline. *Rhino.* New York: Morrow Junior Books, 1995.

Chandler, Gary, and Kevin Graham. *Guardians of Wildlife.* New York: Twenty-First Century Books, 1996.

Croke, Vicki. *The Modern Ark, The Story of Zoos: Past, Present and Future.* New York: Scribner, 1997.

McClung, Robert M. *Last of the Wild: Vanished and Vanishing Giants of the Animal World.* New Haven, Conn.: Linnet Books, 1997.

Nirgiotis, Nicholas, and Theodore Nirgiotis. *No More Dodos: How Zoos Help Endangered Wildlife.* Minneapolis: Lerner Publications Co., 1996.

Penny, Malcolm. *Black Rhino: Habitats, Life Cycle, Food Chains, Threats.* Austin, Tex.: Raintree Steck-Vaughn, 2001.

———. *Endangered Species: Our Impact on the Planet.* Austin, Tex.: Raintree Steck-Vaughn, 2002.

Weintraub, Aileen. *Discovering Africa's Land, People, and Wildlife: A MyReportLinks.com Book.* Berkeley Heights, N.J.: Enslow Publishers, Inc., 2004.